HOW
TO
PLAN
YOUR
OWN
MICROWEDDING

Hey there!

My name's Iver Marjerison, and I am a professional microwedding planner and officiant (and a board game designer, radio host, and writer!). I've had the pleasure of personally planning more than 500 small weddings, and I created this guide as a simple way to share what I've learned. **If for any reason you are not 100% satisfied with the guide, please reach out and I'll make things right.** If you do find it helpful, a positive review on Amazon would be greatly appreciated!

As a wedding professional, I pride myself on offering my services to everyone, regardless of race, ethnicity, religion, sexual orientation, or gender identity. I have tried to write this guide in a way that is helpful and inclusive to all couples. If you have any feedback or questions please reach out.

Cheers,

Iver Marjerison
Founder & Everything Else
MicroWeddings.org
Iver@MicroWeddings.org

P.S. If you want to check out my board game, or other projects, you can find me at IverMarjerison.com. :-)

THIS GUIDE IS BROKEN DOWN INTO FIVE SECTIONS:

INTRO
What are we doing here?

PLACES
Where will the ceremony take place?
What are we doing afterwards for food and drinks?

PEOPLE
Who is going to perform the wedding ceremony?
What about the photographer? Florist? Hair stylist?

CEREMONY
What is the order of events? Should we write our own vows?
Do we need chairs? Or decorations?

LEGAL STUFF
How do we get a marriage licence? What do we do with it?

LITTLE STUFF
What else is there to consider?

PLANNING TOOLKIT
Worksheets and lists to fill out as you go!

INDEX

INTRO

This guide is meant to outline general ideas and suggestions for putting together your own small wedding. Keep in mind that all small weddings are different and will vary by couple, guest count, location, budget, etc. The beauty of a microwedding is the flexibility, so don't get caught up with how it's "supposed" to be. Do what works for you. :-)

How do I use this guide?

This guide is meant to be used in conjunction with my "Planning Toolkit". You will find those resources in the back of this book, but I recommend downloading digital copies as they tend to be easier to work with.

These digital documents can be accessed via:
MicroWeddings.org/toolkit
Password: DIAMONDS
The purchase of this guide gives one individual access to download these digital documents for six months. Please download as soon as possible!

What does a microwedding look like?

You (the couple) and your family and friends will meet at a ceremony location (like a park, beach, etc.) with your officiant and photographer. The officiant, often referred to as the minister, conducts a brief ceremony and completes the marriage license. The photographer takes group photos and then does a short photoshoot with just the two of you. From there, you and your group can head to a local restaurant for dinner and drinks, like a reception. Or, you could hire catering or a private chef to your home or a rental home. Or, you could just have a barbeque!

Technically a group of any size can partake in this more informal wedding style. However, in my experience, groups with more than 30 guests may be more comfortable using a designated event facility (or wedding venue) where they will have a bit more privacy. This better allows for more traditional components like a dance floor and DJ. More info on this in the PLACES section. But remember! This guide is only meant to outline ideas and suggestions for putting together your own small wedding. Keep in mind that all small weddings are different and will vary by couple, guest count, location, budget, etc. The beauty of a microwedding is the flexibility, so don't get caught up with how it's "supposed" to be. Do what works for you. :-)

How do I save money?

We all know, weddings are expensive... But they don't have to be! Microweddings offer a lot of flexibility that traditional weddings do not, with plenty of ways to help get the most out of your budget. I discuss how to find the best value options in the PLACES and PEOPLE sections, but I want to really hammer home my number one piece of advice for saving money...

Avoid "Peak" dates.

There is a MASSIVE difference in demand for wedding vendors and venues based on the day. With this in mind, you can use basic economic principles to determine the best and worst days to try and get good deals. For example, a photographer may have an 8-hour minimum on weekends in June, but might be happy to offer you a 1 hour booking on a Tuesday in April. "Peak" times vary with region, but generally: May-October are the busiest months, Friday/Saturday are the busiest days, and evenings are the busiest time.

What is the simplest way to have a microwedding?

Are you and your fiancé just looking to tie the knot and make things as simple as possible? It's really as easy as this:

> **Step 1:** Call your local County Clerk or government office that issues marriage licenses and ask them what the requirements are. Ask how you can get the marriage license, and how quickly you can return it (some states have a waiting period). Also ask what exactly is required to make it legal. Do you need

an ordained minister? Do you need Witnesses? Once you have the legal stuff figured out, move on to the next step.

Step 2: Find a location for the ceremony, like a local park, mountaintop overlook, or beach.

Step 3: Find a professional officiant and photographer. If you are struggling with Step 2, these vendors may have some recommendations.

Step 4: Meet up with them at the ceremony site, exchange some vows, kiss, get some photos and sign the license... then head somewhere for drinks and cheer!

But I need more help!

Have no fear, I offer a handful of other planning services beyond this guide.

- **"How To Officiate a Wedding" e-guide - $50**
  1-on-1 coaching and resources to help anyone officiate!
  MicroWeddings.org/Coaching

- **Remote Planning Assistance - $50**
  Let's hop on a phone call! I'll help you brainstorm and figure out your day.
  MicroWeddings.org/Remote

- **All-Inclusive MicroWedding Planning - $325ish**
  From the mountaintop, to the photographer and officiant, I'll help you put together every single piece of your day! (Currently only available for weddings in Colorado)
  ColoradoMicroWeddings.com

- **Wedding Officiant - $400 + Travel**
  It would be my absolute honor to officiate your ceremony! I do weddings of all shapes and sizes, and travel anywhere in the world.
  Iver@MicroWeddings.org

- **Blog Posts, Articles, Videos, Podcasts...**
  MicroWeddings.org/Stuff

PLACES

There are typically two components of a microwedding: the ceremony and the dinner/reception. First, I will get into ceremony sites, followed by dinner/reception sites, and finally, a discussion of venues that can do both.

Generally speaking, I have found that it is easiest to have two separate locations, as the ceremony and reception have very different requirements. The most obvious exception to this is going to be your backyard/rental home. However, there are a lot of random exceptions as well, such as a brewery with a private rooftop terrace, a scenic park with a picnic area open for grilling, etc. But generally speaking: it's easier if you don't limit yourself to a location that can handle both the ceremony AND reception.

Ceremony Sites

For your ceremony site, you should look for a location that provides two things: enough space for your group and a nice backdrop for photos. Options are just about endless, but I've listed some of my favorites below, along with detailed descriptions:

- **Parks**: Abundant and accessible, public parks can offer a nice natural setting for a small wedding ceremony. Ideal parks are ones that can offer your group some privacy, or at least an area that is not heavily trafficked (but this is a personal preference). Permits and regulations always vary, so you will need to call the local government agency (like the park district) to inquire about the rules. Generally speaking, a handful of people with an officiant isn't a concern. But if you have a dozen-plus guests and plan to set up chairs and decorations, you may need to acquire a permit.

- **Your backyard**: Assuming there is enough space for your anticipated group size, a backyard wedding offers a simple and affordable option for both privacy and creativity. Unlike a park, you will have more freedom to decorate and are less likely to have to deal with a stranger's dog. As with any event that might include loud music and celebrations, inform your neighbors in advance.

- **Rental homes**: Similar to the personal backyard option, this offers privacy and creative freedom. While searching for home, look for one that has plenty of space for your group size, as well as a nice yard or deck/patio for the ceremony. Be sure to get an "okay" from the host before booking. Definitely be clear that you are planning a small gathering - when homeowners hear "wedding" they immediately think of a large, elaborate, and destructive ordeal. Some rental home websites, like AirBnB, have search filters for event-friendly homes.

- **Wedding Venues**: While wedding venues are typically used for both the ceremony and reception, another option that some wedding venues offer for smaller weddings is the reservation of their ceremony site only. Basically, instead of getting the entire venue for the full day, you would get their ceremony site for a couple of hours. Most venues will not list a package like this on their website, but if you are interested, it never hurts to ask.

- **Indoor options**: If bad weather or personal preference has you shying away from outdoor ceremony sites, there are plenty of indoor alternatives! See the list below for ideas. The biggest objection to an indoor ceremony will be from the photographer, who may worry about poor lighting. So if amazing photos are a priority, you will want to make good lighting a priority. However, you can always do the ceremony indoors, and head somewhere outside afterwards for more photos.

- **Get creative!** Here's a list for inspiration:
    o Mountaintop
    o Aquarium
    o Botanic Gardens
    o Art Gallery
    o Beach
    o Museum
    o Chapel
    o Canyon
    o Brewery
    o House Boat
    o Orchard
    o Winery
    o Historic Building
    o Rooftop Garden

Note: Photographers are usually a wealth of knowledge when it comes to pretty backdrop locations, so if you don't already have a spot in mind, ask for their recommendations!

Dinner/Reception Sites

Generally speaking, if you have less than 30 people, your two primary options are going to be a restaurant or your home/rental home. Much larger, and you may want to include traditional event venues in your search. How to approach each:

- **Restaurants**: I won't go into detail explaining how to find the food you want to eat with your friends and family, but I can tell you that a restaurant that works regularly with groups and parties will likely make your day more comfortable. When you call to make a reservation, ask if they have a private room. If not, inquire how they would set up for a group of your size.

  Keep in mind, unless they state otherwise, a restaurant is not an event venue, and may not accommodate traditional wedding aspects, like the first dance. If you do want more privacy, some restaurants allow you to buy out their entire space for the night. Don't limit yourself strictly to restaurants, as this could also apply to breweries, wineries, etc.

For larger groups, if you plan to pay, and would like to control the total bill, many restaurants will work with you to create a custom menu that limits your guests to predetermined options.

Be sure to have a plan for alcohol as well! Will beer and wine go on the group tab? What about Whiteclaws or shots of Fireball? Added bonus: can the restaurant make the wedding cake for you?!

- **Your home/rental homes**: For obvious reasons, this option offers an affordable and convenient way to eat, drink, and spend time with loved ones. If you're planning something casual, recruiting your aunt to throw some steaks on the grill is always an option.

  But if you want something a little bit more formal, consider a caterer or private chef (or a food truck!). Keep in mind that many restaurants also offer catering-style takeout options for group dining. When getting quotes, be sure to inquire about guest count minimums.

  As always, if you're working with a rental home, be sure to get the "okay" from the host, and familiarize yourself with their kitchen and dining amenities (is there enough chairs, counter space, etc.?).

- **Event spaces**: Not the norm for a smaller wedding, but if you are looking to do some dancing and want the feel of a traditional wedding reception, an event space may be the best option. As I will explain below, you are not necessarily looking specifically for a wedding reception venue. Instead, think of public event spaces or restaurant banquet rooms. Some of the best options are city-owned event facilities.

Unlike traditional wedding venues, many of these spaces allow you to bring in your own bartender, booze, and dining services that fit your preference and budget.

Traditional Wedding Venues

And then of course, there are traditional wedding venues. These are event spaces specifically designed for an elegant ceremony site alongside a space to wine and dine. Unfortunately, these locations are rarely financially feasible for small groups due to their pricing minimums. If you do have your sights set on something like this, I would consider planning on a Monday through Thursday date. If a wedding venue is going to work with the budget and needs of a small group, they are more likely to be flexible on their slow days! Also, consider an off-season wedding (November through April), or something in the morning. But really, it is all about your budget. If the venue has a minimum guest count of 50, they aren't going to turn down your group of 20 if you are okay with paying the same price.

Again, most wedding venues are going to have ceremony and reception packages combined. But some might be flexible, especially if you are working with them on an off-day, or during off-season. If you have a spot in mind for the ceremony, but need a spot to celebrate afterwards (or vice versa), it may be worth reaching out to some local venues to see if they can accommodate you!

PEOPLE

Wedding vendors - think officiant, photographer, hair stylist, etc. - are the lifeblood of your wedding day. They will provide all the pieces you need to make your wedding a success. You can hire just one (the officiant) or all nine that are listed below. But for a microwedding, the two most common are the officiant and photographer.

Finding Your Vendors

As with most things, an online search is the first step. Scout options, compare prices, and shoot some emails. In this field, reviews are everything. Find people with proven track records. It's best to first reach out via email, but to find out for sure if someone is a good fit, ask to hop on a phone call.

Keep in mind that wedding vendors cross paths often, so once you find one good vendor feel free to ask them for suggestions. Officiants almost always know photographers to recommend, for instance.

Vendor Directories

Weddingwire.com and TheKnot.com (Best options)

These are the most popular wedding vendor sites and will generally feature the more experienced options. The most expensive photographers in your state will likely be on these websites, but that doesn't mean the microwedding photographer of your dreams isn't on there as well! Oftentimes, getting listed on the first page of the search results is prohibitively expensive for vendors who work with small weddings, so you may have to flip through a few pages to find the right fit. It should be relatively clear what vendors are accommodating of small weddings, for example, if a photographer lists a minimum package of 8 hours, they likely aren't what you're looking for.

Thumbtack.com and Craigslist.com

These sites aren't wedding specific and will generally have more affordable and less experienced options. That's not to say there aren't some incredibly talented photographers on Craigslist. Just keep in mind there may be more risk involved with these sites. Always look at photos and read reviews. Rule of thumb: if a vendor quotes you dramatically less than the next cheapest option you have found, seriously consider their qualifications.

Yelp.com, Google, etc.

With websites and search engines that don't specialize in wedding vendors, it can often be difficult to pick up the signal from the noise. With Google in particular, you will likely find your searches gummed up by traditional wedding vendors and venues, whose packages and prices will likely not be what you are looking for. Try using specific keywords like: "Elopement", "Microwedding", etc. Ever since COVID-19, there has been a massive increase in the amount of vendors who cater specifically to this style of wedding.

Individuals vs. Companies

During your search, you will find that some vendors work independently or for themselves (I.e. "Dave's Photography"), and others are part of a company (i.e. "Nevada Party DJs"). As a rule of thumb, the companies are going to be more expensive, but that doesn't mean they should necessarily be avoided. There are many small collectives of hair and makeup stylists, for instance, that are able to provide quality and reasonable prices, with the added assurance of a larger team. For example, if your booked stylist were to get sick, someone else would easily be able to fill in. Be wary of national companies with pricing that seems too good to be true. Building a beautiful website and then sending out (and underpaying) inexperienced photographers/DJs/etc. is a popular business strategy.

Special Concern for Small Weddings

One of the biggest concerns vendors have with booking "small weddings" is their opportunity cost. A professional wedding photographer will likely turn down a one-hour microwedding job on a Saturday evening in June (even if they currently have the date open), because the likelihood of booking a larger, more lucrative wedding for that same date and time is very high. For this reason, your vendor search may be much easier if you are able to work with one of these three "off-peak" criteria: Monday-Thursday, mornings, or November-April.

Email Inquiry Templates

I've included an email template for each of the primary vendors. These are generalized for a typical microwedding. You may find that your specific situation would benefit from providing or asking for additional information or the removal of certain elements. Just keep in mind that the goal when reaching out to a vendor is to provide enough information that they are 1) able to determine if they are a good fit, and 2) provide you with a quote.

Remember to cast a wide net! Sending out inquiries to a bunch of photographers at one time is the best way to find one that will work.

If you don't know the exact date, time, or location of your ceremony yet, you can still reach out to vendors. Just give them a general idea of what you are considering. Being flexible on dates while looking for vendors can actually be helpful. You may find yourself in a situation where the photographer and officiant that you want are not available for the same Saturday, but would both be available on Sunday.

Wedding vendors all think about opportunity cost. If you reach out to all the top videographers in your area requesting them to book a Saturday evening in June for a one-hour gig, you are going to get a lot of disappointing replies. If you aren't able to pay these premiums (or just get lucky), remember that trying to book smaller packages on weekdays, mornings, and/or off-season dates is going to be a lot more appealing for vendors.

I highly recommend accessing the digital version of the email templates so you can copy and paste them into your emails!
MicroWeddings.org/toolkit
Password: DIAMONDS

The Vendors

Here's a list of the most common wedding vendors, followed by a list with detailed descriptions of each and what you should know when looking for them:

Officiant
Photographer
Videographer
Florist
Bakery
Hair and Makeup Stylist
Catering/Private Chef
Music/DJ
Bartender
Rentals
Day-of Coordinator

Note: This list is not exhaustive, and there are all different kinds of vendors you may want to hire for your wedding, but these are the most common.

Officiant

As the officiant performs the wedding ceremony, they are essentially the only required vendor. Traditionally, most people associate wedding officiants with ministers, but today all kinds of people officiate weddings of all styles. Any professional wedding officiant will hold the necessary criteria to legally solemnize your marriage and provide instruction regarding the marriage license process. Although in many cases, couples can handle the legal part on their own at the courthouse and then simply have a symbolic ceremony.

Another option is to have a friend or family member officiate the ceremony. If you are interested in this option, I offer an officiant guide and coaching for $50. Visit this link for more information: MicroWeddings.org/coaching

As they are the ones that will write the ceremony script, your officiant will set the style and mood of your ceremony. Many officiants are flexible, but most have a style that they are going to be more comfortable with. If you are looking for something more traditional, seek out an officiant that describes their services this way. Likewise, if you are looking for something more contemporary, look for an officiant that describes their services as more casual or modern. One of the primary variables in a wedding is choosing if you'd like a religious or a secular (non-religious) ceremony. Either way, talk to your officiant to make sure you are both on the same page, and that they are comfortable catering to your needs.

Most importantly, the officiant is going to be standing beside you on one of the most important days of your life, so find someone that you vibe with! Speaking as an officiant, I can say that there is nothing more valuable than getting on a quick phone call to get a real feel for each other.

For the "Style of ceremony," you will want to mention if you are looking for something more traditional or something more contemporary. Also let them know if you would like a secular (non-religious) or religious ceremony, and if there are any other specific cultural elements you know you would like to add. Some officiants charge more to have them attend the rehearsal. This is generally not needed, but it is best to let them know up front if you would like them there.

Officiant Email

Hey there!

I am planning a simple "micro-wedding" and am currently looking for an officiant. Here are the details:

Ceremony date:
Ceremony time:
Ceremony location:
Guest count:
Style of ceremony:
Needed for rehearsal:

Are you available for this day? Do you have any specific packages that fit a wedding like this? If you are not available, any recommendations for an officiant that would be a good fit?

Thank you for your time!

Photographer

If you are lucky enough to have a friend or family member who is a professional wedding photographer, that could be a great way to save money! However, if you have an uncle who just happens to have a nice camera, I would recommend sourcing professionally. This not only makes for better photos, but frees up your loved ones to relax and enjoy the day.

When finding a photographer, search the usual wedding directories but don't forget about social media. Instagram is a great way to browse different photographers and get a feel for your preferred style. But keep in mind what your setting is going to be. A photographer with epic mountain photos, might not be the best fit for your indoor ceremony. And don't get tricked by the highlight reel! If their portfolio doesn't have a lot of photos, ask to see a FULL wedding album. If you are trusting them to capture your day, make sure you know and love their work.

The amount of photography you'll need is up to you. For a microwedding, it's most common to have the photographer shoot the ceremony, group/family shots, and a couple's portrait session. For that, you shouldn't need more than 1-2 hours of the photographer's time. Not having your photographer be present for the "getting ready" and reception photos is a great way to save money. But if you decide you do want these moments captured, most photographers will work with you to put together a package that suits you. Most wedding photographers list packages in the 6+ hour range, but this doesn't mean that they won't do something smaller.

Photographer Email

Hey there!

I am planning a simple "micro-wedding" and am currently looking for a photographer. Here are the details:

Ceremony date:
Ceremony time:
Ceremony location:
Guest count:
Photography needed:

Are you available for this day? Do you have any specific packages that fit a wedding like this? Do your packages include the rights to the digital photos or would we have to pay additionally after the wedding?

If you are not available, any recommendations for a photographer that would be a good fit?

Thank you for your time!

Note: If you aren't sure how many hours of photography you need, tell them what you have in mind and let them make a suggestion for the time needed. For example: "Photography needed: We would like to do a first look before the ceremony, and then do a few group/family photos after, and then maybe have 45 minutes with just the two of us... we don't need any getting ready or reception photos."

Videographer

Most wedding videographers do massive weddings, record hours of footage, and charge a small fortune. However, there are some who offer "elopement-style" packages that are perfect for microweddings. This style of work is simple, affordable, and still provides a magical way to remember your day. If you want a cinematic video with music and artistic editing, this is your best option. If you really just want a stationary video of the ceremony, a friend or family member's iPhone should be able to do the job (but consider investing in some kind of microphone/audio recorder).

When in search of a videographer for your microwedding, try searching for "elopement videography." If that doesn't work, take the same approach as photography. Search on the wedding directory sites and social media to find someone who fits your style, then simply ask if they are willing to work with your day. Generally speaking, you'll want at least two hours (to cover the ceremony, group/family shots, and couple's portrait session), but in some cases one hour may suffice.

Fair warning: videographers have a much higher financial and time investment required for each event that they do, regardless of the size. You should reasonably expect to pay at least twice the amount that you might pay for your photographer.

Videographer Email

Hey there!

I am planning a simple "micro-wedding" and am currently looking for a videographer. Here are the details:

Ceremony date:
Ceremony time:
Ceremony location:
Guest count:
Videography needed:

Are you available for this day? Do you have any specific packages that fit a wedding like this? If you are not available, any recommendations for a videographer that would be a good fit?

Thank you for your time!

Note: If you aren't sure how many hours of videography you need, tell them what you have in mind and let them make a suggestion for the time needed. For example: "Videography needed: We would like you to cover a first look before the ceremony, the ceremony, and our couple's photoshoot which should be about 45 minutes... we don't need any coverage of getting ready or the reception."

Florist

Find a few florists with good reviews in your area and check out their photos to get a feel for their style. Oftentimes, the website may be highly curated, so look for photos shared by customers, if possible. When you reach out to them for quotes, be sure to send photos of what you have in mind. Tell them SPECIFICALLY what you like about the bouquet photos you send.

Alternatively, there are some surprisingly great bouquets made of dried and/or fake flowers available on Etsy and Amazon! Another option is to simply buy a bouquet from a local grocery store. However, you may want to cut off the bottom and wrap it with ribbon for a more polished look. Oh, and don't forget the boutonniere - the flower generally worn by the groom, or on a suit jacket.

Flower needs vary with wedding size and style. Most common for microweddings are bouquets for brides and boutonnieres for grooms. Many smaller weddings don't have bridesmaids or groomsmen, so you don't have to worry about their flowers. If you do plan to have a bridal party standing up with you, adjust accordingly.

Bouquets are not one-size-fits-all, and each florist does them a bit differently. If you want something more budget-friendly and still elegant, consider requesting a quote for a "bridesmaid" bouquet, instead of a "bridal" bouquet.

Florist Email

Hey there!

I am planning a simple "micro-wedding" and am currently looking for flowers. Here are the details:

Ceremony date:
Ceremony time:
Ceremony location:
Guest count:
Flowers needed:
Notes on attached photos:
If you are able to do these arrangements, can I get a quote? Is it possible to have the flowers delivered, or would we have to pick them up?

If you are not available, any recommendations for a florist that would be a good fit?

Thank you for your time!

Note: Let them know what kind of arrangements you need. For example: "Flowers needed: One bridal bouquet, two bridesmaid bouquets, three boutonnières." Also, it's best to attach a few photos for inspiration, and to tell them what you specifically like most about the photos you share. If you are looking for a more budget-friendly bridal bouquet, ask to get one that is bridesmaid-sized.

Bakery

Look online for photos of wedding cakes that you like. Once you have an idea, reach out to local bakeries with example photos. A great way to save money, and add a touch of personalization, is to get the cake without decor, then add your own topper and/or flowers. There are a lot of beautiful, unique cake toppers on Etsy, and your florist will be able to provide some matching flowers (they know the foodsafe ones) to decorate with. Another economic and simple option is to get a cake from a local grocery store. You may be surprised at the selections they offer! Hint: Whole Foods' chantilly cake is my go-to suggestion for simple and beautiful.

Note that *wedding-height* cakes are taller than regular cakes, and look better in photos. The smallest cake that still has multiple tiers or levels generally feeds 25 people. So if your group is smaller than that, you will likely want a single-tier cake... unless you'd like a lot of leftovers!

But remember - you don't have to have a traditional cake. Cupcakes, donut walls, and macarons are all cool options as well!

Bakery Email

Hey there!

I am planning a simple "micro-wedding" and am currently looking for a wedding cake. Here are the details:

Ceremony date:
Ceremony time:
Ceremony location:
Guest count:
Cake flavor/type:
Notes on attached photos:

If you are able to do this, can I get a suggestion on a cake size to feed my group, as well as a quote? Is it possible to have the cake delivered, or would we have to pick it up?

If you are not available, any recommendations for a bakery that would be a good fit?

Thank you for your time!

Note: It's hard to know what size cake you need to feed a particular group size, so it's best to just provide guest count and let them make a suggestion. If you have something specific in mind, provide photos and let them know what you like and don't like about them. It's also good to mention cake/ frosting flavor preferences and any other relevant details.

Hair and Makeup Stylist

This vendor may not specialize in weddings, so searching local hair salons may be as effective as looking for a designated "wedding stylist." As with most vendors, during your research you should look for good reviews and photos that match your style.

Many stylists do hair OR makeup, so if you can find someone that does both, it generally is going to make your day easier and save you some money. An added bonus is if you can find a stylist who will travel to wherever you are getting ready on the day of the wedding. Most wedding specific stylists offer this service, but many salons do as well.

Warning: Based on my purely unscientific anecdotal experience, the stylist is by far the most likely vendor to arrive late or cancel last minute. Read reviews carefully, and get the best that your budget can afford.

Hair and Makeup Stylist Email

Hey there!

I am planning a simple "micro-wedding" and am currently looking for a stylist. Here are the details:

Ceremony date:
Ceremony time:
Ceremony location:
Guest count:
Services needed:

If you are able to do this, can I get a quote? Are you able to travel to us, or would we have to come to your salon?

If you are not available, any recommendations for a stylist that would be a good fit?

Thank you for your time!

Note: Let them know how many people and what exactly you have in mind. For example: "Services needed: Hair and makeup for myself and my mom, and hair for my maid of honor." Keep in mind, many stylists only do hair OR makeup. If you find yourself reaching out to someone for one, inquire about a recommendation for the other.

Catering/Private Chef

If you plan to have the reception at your home or a rental home, this can be a good option. These professionals tend to be the easiest to find on Yelp or Google Business. However, while many are happy to work with smaller groups, others will have minimum guest counts, so be sure to find out asap when shopping around. Another option to consider is catering-style takeout from restaurants or grocery stores. Hint: If you're looking for crowd-pleasing, budget-minding deliciousness, it's hard to beat Chipotle!

Catering/Private Chef Email

Hey there!

I am planning a simple "micro-wedding" and am currently looking for food options. Here are the details:

Ceremony date:
Ceremony time:
Ceremony location:
Meal time:
Meal location:
Guest count:
Food needed:

Do you have any sample menus that would work for this? If you are able to do this, can I get a quote?

If you are not available, any recommendations for another option that would be a good fit?

Thank you for your time!

Note: This is one that is going to vary greatly from group to group. Consider things like what you will need food for (cocktail hour, dinner, dessert, etc.), the style of food you want, how you want it served, if you need them to help set up/clean up, and if you need utensils, plating, etc.

Live Music/DJ

If your wedding is going to be a casual celebration with 30 of your closest friends and family, you probably won't need a DJ. Still, that doesn't mean your special day needs to be devoid of music. Hiring a live guitarist for the ceremony, or having a friend man a bluetooth speaker for the processional/ recessional, are both ideal for intimate settings (more details on this option can be found in the CEREMONY section).

If you go the live music route, I recommend searching Gigmasters.com or any of the usual wedding directories. Live musicians tend to range widely by price, so definitely shop around. For a small wedding, you may need less than a full hour of music, so be sure to relay your vision for the day so they understand the simplicity of your needs. Expect most musicians to have at least a 1 hour minimum though.

If you plan to have a reception with a dance floor, even for a small wedding, you may want to find a DJ. Running a playlist on Spotify is never quite the same energy catalyst that a DJ provides. Plus, DJs don't just control the music - they usually orchestrate the timing of the whole evening and keep things running smoothly. The exception would be if you find yourself about to hire the cheapest DJ in your area. In my professional experience, low-quality DJs are the same or sometimes worse than your uncle's Spotify-manning abilities. This is another vendor that has a high overhead cost regardless of wedding size, so don't be surprised if the experienced ones aren't willing to cut you a massive deal.

Warning: For various reasons (that I'd be happy to discuss over a beer sometime) there are a lot of poor quality DJs in the wedding industry. A bad DJ is worse than no DJ, in my opinion. So while there are corners that can be cut to save money, the DJ is not one that I recommend (more stories best told over a beer). Read reviews carefully, and get the best that your budget can afford.

Music/DJ Email

Hey there!

I am planning a simple "micro-wedding" and am currently looking for music options. Here are the details:

Ceremony date:
Ceremony time:
Ceremony location:
Guest count:
Services needed:

If you are able to do this, can I get a quote?

If you are not available, any recommendations for another option that would be a good fit?

Thank you for your time!

Note: If you also need music for the reception, provide that information as well. Keep in mind, a traditional wedding generally has a DJ for 6-8 hours, while a simple microwedding might only need a guitarist for 30-60 minutes for the ceremony. If you are doing an outdoor ceremony, be sure to get information regarding how they handle bad weather.

Bartender

Even if you're just having a casual dinner/reception in your backyard, hiring a bartender can be a cool way to add atmosphere to the event. In many cases, they will provide things like mixers and bar equipment, and will assist with sourcing the alcohol (or you may be able to buy your own for them to serve). Some may even buy back extra alcohol at the end of the night, which is nice, because guesstimating the amount of alcohol that a large group is going to consume can be difficult.

If you are getting a caterer, ask them for bartender recommendations. If not, a simple google should provide a plethora of choices. No need to search for a wedding-specific option.

If you do end up using an event space that allows BYO, they will more than likely require that you have insurance of some kind. Oftentimes, the bartending company will handle this for you.

Bartender Email

Hey there!

I am planning a simple "micro-wedding" and am currently looking for a bartender. Here are the details:

Ceremony date:
Ceremony time:
Ceremony location:
Reception time:
Reception location:
Guest count:
Services needed:

If you are able to do this, can I get a quote? Are you able to provide things like mixers, glassware, alcohol, etc.? Or are we responsible for that?

If you are not available, any recommendations for a bartender that would be a good fit?

Thank you for your time!

Note: Generally speaking, if you are able to provide your own alcohol, it is going to be cheaper, but some bartending services offer a buyback, which means if you overestimate how much alcohol you need, they will buy it back from you at the end of the night. If you are also doing a caterer, you should ask if they provide bartending services first, to keep things simple.

Rentals

Rentals can include things like chairs, tents, arches, etc. Many microweddings don't require these things, but I go into a little more detail about who may want/need them in the CEREMONY section.

If you do decide you'd like to rent something, simple google searches like "wedding arch rental" or "white folding chair rental" (plus your area) should return the best and easiest options. Conveniently, many of these vendors have photo catalogs of their specific rentals on their websites, so you can easily browse and find what you are looking for. I always recommend white chairs of some kind as they tend to look the best in photos.

Note that many of these companies will offer the option to deliver and set up your rental for an additional fee. Though it's tempting to just pick up and set up yourself, I highly recommend paying extra for delivery/set up, if it works with your budget. It's a massive convenience and one less thing to worry about on your big day.

Rentals Email

Hey there!

I am planning a simple "micro-wedding" and am currently looking for some rentals. Here are the details:

Ceremony date:
Ceremony time:
Ceremony location:
Guest count:
Rentals needed:

If you are able to do this, can I get a quote with set up and delivery and without?

If you are not available, any recommendations for another rental option that would be a good fit?

Thank you for your time!

Note: Almost every rental company is going to have an online catalog showing their different options. It's best to familiarize yourself with this so you can ask for the specific type of rental when you reach out to them. You will likely find that the individual cost of renting something, like chairs for example, is relatively cheap, but the fees for delivery and setup can get more expensive. While it may be tempting not to, I highly recommend paying extra to have them deliver and set up, if it fits within your budget.

Day-of Coordinator

While it's all about your style, in my experience, weddings with less than 20 people generally don't need a coordinator present on the day of the wedding (especially if you have a professional, and helpful, officiant and photographer).

However, if you do decide you need a professional onhand, I suggest looking for a local day-of coordinator who has an assistant that might provide a more budget-friendly package for your small wedding. This is simply because traditional wedding coordinators tend to be very protective of their days and are unlikely to accommodate for smaller wedding budgets. However, COVID-19 has resulted in a massive increase in wedding planners offering elopement and microwedding packages, so it's definitely worth looking around to see what people are offering in your area!

These wedding vendors use a lot of different titles (i.e. planner, coordinator, consultant), but basically for a microwedding you are looking for someone who can be there the day of the wedding to be the contact person for the vendors, help decorate and set up, help put out fires (i.e. lost rings, broken heels, etc.), and lend you some peace of mind. They will also work with you beforehand to create the timeline, discuss bad weather contingency plans, and provide general insight from a professional.

Day-of Coordinator Email

Hey there!

I am planning a simple "micro-wedding" and am currently looking for a day-of coordinator. Here are the details:

Ceremony date:
Ceremony time:
Ceremony location:
Guest count:
Day-of hours needed:

I am putting together the primary components of my day, including the venue and vendors. But, I would like someone to help me go over the little stuff to make sure I haven't missed anything, as well as be present the day of the wedding to make sure everything runs smoothly.

Are you available for this date? Do you have any specific packages that fit these needs?

If you are not available, any recommendations for a coordinator that would be a good fit?

Thank you for your time!

Note: This is another one that is going to change a lot from wedding to wedding. In this email, the more information you can provide about your ceremony and reception, the better. It's also important to be clear about what work you have already done, and what you still need help with.

CEREMONY

In many ways, a microwedding ceremony is like a traditional wedding: a happy couple up front with an officiant, while friends and family look on fondly. The main differences are the size and the setting. Instead of guests filling the pews of a church, the ceremony described below might take place with guests standing together in the corner of a city park.

Your ceremony script will be written by your officiant, but you can typically work with them if you have something specific in mind. Generally, you can expect a microwedding ceremony to be between 8-20 minutes.

Order of Events

Each ceremony is a bit different, but here is the general order of events:

1. **Processional**: For a super simple microwedding, the couple typically starts up front with the officiant, with the groom on the officiant's left and the bride on the officiant's right (when the officiant is facing the guests). No family or bridal party walks down the aisle. The most common variation would be to have the groom and officiant start up front, and to have the bride walk down the aisle, with or without an escort - usually with music playing! For a more traditional approach, the groom and officiant can walk down first, followed by any family members you'd like to include (i.e. parents, grandparents), bridesmaids and groomsmen (typically with the groomsmen on the bridesmaids' right arms), the ringbearer, the flower girl, and finally, the bride. If you are two brides, two grooms, or nonbinary... or if you just don't like traditions, feel free to have people walk in any order, and stand wherever you want. :-)

If you google processional orders, you will find everyone does it a bit differently. With something more elaborate, you'll want one song for everyone before the bride, and a second song just for her. If you're not hiring a DJ or live musician, a guest manning a bluetooth speaker works just fine. Details on this option can be found in this section under "Music."

2. **Ceremony**: The officiant, the bride, the groom, and any bridal party are now all standing up front. Again, the bride is typically to the officiant's right, and the groom is to the officiant's left, though this is not required (obviously). The music has stopped, and the officiant begins the ceremony. If there are chairs, the officiant will ask the guests to sit before beginning. Officiants are responsible for writing the ceremony, so you shouldn't have to worry much about that. They will likely walk you through their ceremony flow, but the primary components include: introduction, vows, ring exchange, "I dos", and the kiss. They will also work with you if you'd like to incorporate other cultural/religious elements (prayer or poem reading, sand ceremony, etc.).

3. **Recessional**: The couple, followed by the bridal party, walk back down the aisle. It's also nice to have a song play for this as well. For larger groups, the officiant will direct the guests where to go.

4. **Celebrate**: From here, the couple generally starts exchanging hugs and high fives with loved ones, before transitioning into group/family photos, and the license signing.

Vows

Again, details of the ceremony and what you would like included are things you will work out with your officiant. But typically you can repeat vows after the officiant, or write your own vows. If you don't want to write your own "vows" exactly, but would like to say something, you can ask your officiant to work "love letters" into the ceremony. A love letter is an open-ended opportunity for you to say anything you want. Things like, "On our first date, you spilled ice cream on yourself, and that's when I knew," etc. Following love letters, you can then repeat more traditional vows after the officiant. Love letters are a great way to say something nice to each other, without stressing about the constricting nature of "vows." Again, there are no set rules, so it's really up to you and your officiant how things will go.

First Look

Traditionally, on the day of the wedding the couple sees each other for the first time at the "altar". But I've found that this can be logistically difficult for small weddings, and it also takes away from a really cool photography opportunity. Before the ceremony, I've found it's best to have the bride/groom placed somewhere near the ceremony site, and then have the bride/groom walk up and tap her/him on the shoulder. They then turn around and see each other for the first time that day and have a nice moment together as the photographer takes photos. That way, some of the butterflies can calm down before the ceremony and your first time seeing each other can feel a little more intimate (and you get some awesome photos!).

Music

If you have a DJ or live musician, they will take the lead on this and work with you to plan what songs will be played and when. If you don't have either of these vendors, I highly recommend setting up a simple music option on your own. This can be as easy as bringing a bluetooth speaker connected to someone's phone with a specific playlist ready to go. Make sure the person in charge of the music has a charged phone, a charged speaker, the playlist downloaded, and specific directions regarding when to start/stop the music.

For a typical full processional, a song should start as soon as the first person begins walking down the aisle, and plays until everyone gets down the aisle, except the bride. At this point, the first song should be faded out, and the bride's song should begin. Once the bride reaches the front, her song should be faded out. Then the officiant can begin. After the couple kisses and the officiant introduces them, a fun recessional song can be played as well.

Even if you are not having a full processional, walking down the aisle in silence is not recommended, and you can easily just have one nice song playing for the bride/groom walk. Remember, no rules!

Chairs

Whether or not you want chairs will depend on your group size and the style you're going for. In my experience, groups of 20 or less people really don't need seating. If you have some elderly guests who will need to sit for the 10-minute ceremony, you can easily bring a few chairs for them. Alternatively, if you want more of a traditional wedding feel, you can rent white folding chairs from a local company. I recommend paying the extra fee for the chairs to be delivered and set up for you so you don't have to deal with it. Just make sure that wherever you are doing the ceremony allows this! Some parks and national forest land do not allow you to set up infrastructure, but will allow you to have a ceremony without it.

Decorations

If your microwedding involves a dozen people gathering at a local park to do a 10-minute ceremony, you may not need much for decorations. If you're creating a more styled setting, you can decorate chairs with fake flowers, or work with your florist to decorate with real flowers. Another element to help create a wedding feel, is an arch for the couple to stand in front of during the ceremony, which can also be decorated with flowers.

If you are doing a more traditional reception, you will most likely want some decorations, such as centerpieces for the tables, a table with a guest book and some photos of the couple, etc. This sort of traditional wedding decor is out of the scope of this guide, but Pinterest is filled with ideas for decorations.

Planning for Weather

Rain, snow, sleet, volcanic eruption... it's hard to know what will happen, but you should make sure to have a plan! Almost all traditional wedding venues have an indoor backup option for outdoor ceremonies. But as you know, most microweddings are not held at these sorts of venues.

If you are doing your microwedding somewhere like a park, you may be tempted to find a covered picnic area or pavilion to use as a bad-weather backup. These can work, but generally speaking, they are often very unphotogenic. In many cases, you might not even have one nearby. So, if you do happen to have a beautiful pavilion close to your site - that's great! But if not - that's okay too! About 95% of the weddings I plan with my company in Colorado do not have an indoor backup.

In my experience, a little rain and snow can be easily managed as long as guests come prepared with umbrellas and warm clothing... and in fact the photos can often turn out really cool!

The big thing to remember is: you are not a group of 100+ people who need to set up a lawn full of seating or extravagant decorations. The beauty of microweddings is the flexibility and mobility. Maybe you can push the ceremony back 30 minutes to avoid the worst of the storm. Maybe you'll need to warm up in the car for a few minutes before you jump into the group photos.

Just be sure to keep checking the weather starting a few days before the big day, and have umbrellas - or whatever else is available - to mitigate potential issues.

When planning, it is useful to look up the average weather for your location and date. Here's a helpful link: Weatherspark.com.

Also, be sure you are aware of how adverse weather could affect your day-of vendors. For example, photographers can generally work in the rain, but violinists cannot.

A Note For Large Groups:
If you have a group of 40+ people, plan to do a lot of decorating, and/or really hate being cold/wet, I would suggest scrapping all of the info above and finding a ceremony site that is either indoors, or that offers an indoor backup option.

LEGAL STUFF

The first thing you should know is that *the ceremony itself is not
inherently a legal process*. The legal part is **obtaining, signing,
and filing the marriage license**, which you can often do with or
without a ceremony.

Which means, even though cartoon Daffy Duck is not legally able
to sign a marriage license, you could still have him officiate your
ceremony. But, of course, nothing would legally change until you
get the marriage license taken care of (which could be done
before, or at a later time).

I mention this separation of the symbolic and legal components of
marriage, because, in many cases it can be more convenient for
the couple.

For example: if the couple wants to be legally married for various
governmental reasons next month, but they'd like to do the
ceremony next fall. Or, perhaps the couple is doing the ceremony
in a different state, but would prefer to take care of the legal stuff
in their own state.

In any case, for the actual legal process, defer to your wedding
officiant to walk you through the requirements, as they do vary
state to state. For example, some states require the couple to
verbally say "I do," while others just require the license to be

signed. If you don't have an officiant yet, or don't plan to use one, simply call/email the governing body (generally the "County Clerk") in the area who is responsible for issuing marriage licenses.

Marriage License

Typically in the US, couples applying for a marriage license must go in person to a county clerk's office to complete an application and show identification. In some cases, you will get the license on the spot, and it can be used immediately, while other states have a mailing process and/or required waiting period.

Once you have the license, you will normally fill it out with your officiant after the ceremony (some states require witness signatures as well, some don't), and then file it with the county clerk. Some officiants may offer to file it for you.

In some cases, like Colorado, the couple is able to "self-solemnize," meaning they can walk into the county clerk's office, fill out some paperwork, and be married within 20 minutes. Then, if they want to have a symbolic ceremony the following day, they can do so without worrying about the legal stuff.

Getting Married in Another State

Every state in the US recognizes marriage licenses from all other states, and does not restrict the application process to residents. Meaning, if you are from Nebraska, but are traveling to Colorado for your wedding, you can get a Colorado marriage license when you get there. Some states will allow you to use their marriage license in a different state, while others require that their license be used for a wedding within the state. Again, your officiant should be able to answer these questions for you.

Having a Friend Officiate

Here's a helpful link that outlines the requirements of the officiant state by state: https://theamm.org/minister-registration

Again, if you are having a friend or family member officiate, I provide a bunch of tips, info, and 1-on-1 coaching with my $50 "How To Officiate a Wedding" e-guide. More info can be found at: MicroWeddings.org/Coaching

LITTLE STUFF

Take it or leave it – here is some little stuff you may want to consider!

First Dance, Cake Cutting, Toasts, etc.

Just because you are having a microwedding, that doesn't mean you have to miss out on every part of a traditional wedding. You might just have to get a little creative. For instance, let's say you are having a ceremony in a park and then going to a restaurant for dinner. Since a lot of restaurants aren't set up for a "dance," you can have your first dance right in the park! Following the ceremony, you can simply have your song play through a bluetooth speaker and have your first dance right there, still surrounded by your loved ones. Plus, it makes for great photos! :-)

Likewise, cake cutting and toasts are two other common wedding aspects that can usually be accommodated for in most settings - just run it by the restaurant first! As always, it will depend on your unique situation, but don't count anything out.

Rehearsal Dinner

Traditionally, a rehearsal dinner takes place the day before the wedding, when the bridal party does a practice walk-through of the processional and recessional of the ceremony, followed by a dinner. For larger weddings, it is super helpful to have the bridal party figure out where they are supposed to stand and who they will walk with, among other things. For smaller weddings, a rehearsal is often not needed.

The rehearsal does not need to be at the actual ceremony location - any open space should work. You should have everyone in the processional (like the groom, family members, bridal party, bride, etc.) line up and practice their walks down the "aisle" in the planned order, making sure everyone knows where they are standing or sitting after they get to the "altar." You do not need any of the vendors (like the officiant) present for the rehearsal. It is not a full walk-through of the ceremony, but rather the processional and the recessional walking orders.

A rehearsal dinner also helps prevent guests who are traveling for the wedding from sitting around the hotel room by themselves the night before. For a smaller wedding with a very simple processional/recessional, you may not need to rehearse, but it might still be nice to plan a dinner for the night before. You can still call it your rehearsal dinner if you want. ;-)

Lodging

Your lodging needs and options will depend greatly on where you are going and what your group is like. In general, hotels tend to be the most accommodating lodging option for groups of different sizes and budgets. If you end up needing more than 10 hotel rooms, call and see if you can get a group discount rate.

However, if you are traveling, and even if most of the group will need hotel rooms, a rental home (like an AirBnB or VRBO) for part of the group (such as immediate family, bridal party, etc.) can be a nice option. That way, the bride and the groom and immediate family and friends have a communal place to congregate and get ready before the ceremony. It also creates a sort of hub for the weekend and a place where everyone can hang out, eat, drink, and socialize.

When scouting for group lodging options, consider the amenities as much as the location. Having a hotel or rental home that is close to the ceremony and reception site(s) is a huge convenience. Additionally, having your group somewhere with dining and entertainment options nearby can make for a more enjoyable weekend.

Weekend Plans

With a large wedding and 15 second-cousins to deal with, keeping everyone entertained quickly becomes a very hands-on activity.

However, no matter what the size of your group is, you may want to have some options in mind for group activities. Most people know the value of planning a nice dinner for the night before the wedding, but planning a breakfast the morning after the wedding (french toast? Bloody mary bar?!) is often overlooked, but just as fun.

Beyond dining, think about what your area has to offer and what your group likes to do. GroupOn.com is a great way to find activities you might not think of! Topgolf is also always a winner, as well as arcade bars like Dave & Buster's, or sporting events, water parks, horse races, monster truck shows, trampoline parks, boat rentals... the list goes on and on. :-)

Timing

If you are doing an outdoor ceremony and are prioritizing the quality of your photos, a photographer worth their weight will urge you to opt for sunrise or sunset. Typically, ideal sunrise lighting starts ten minutes before technical sunrise time. Sunset lighting, often called golden hour, is estimated as the hour before the technical sunset time. There will be variations on this, so be sure to consult your photographer. To check the exact sunrise and sunset for your date and location, simply Google: "Sunset [your date] [your location]". That being said, good photographers can still create really nice photos at other times of the day. However, it is best to avoid the harsh lighting of the middle of the day, about 11 am to 2 pm.

Emergency Kit

On the day of the wedding, it's really helpful to have a bag full of items that may come in handy in a pinch. I recommend preparing the bag in advance and adding items as they come to mind. You can find my recommended items on the WORKSHEET, but it includes things like umbrellas, clothes pins, bobby pins, stain remover, lint roller, etc.

PLANNING TOOLKIT

On the following pages you will find the these resources to help you plan your day. You should work through the TO-DO LIST, as you fill out the WORKSHEET, while referencing this GUIDE BOOK for detailed information.

The digital version of these documents can be accessed via:
MicroWeddings.org/toolkit
Password: DIAMONDS
The purchase of this guide gives one individual access to download these digital documents for six months. So please download as soon as possible! Any issues please email me:
Iver@Microweddings.org

A: To-Do List
From brainstorming to the kiss, this is a step-by-step list of the things that need to get done.

B: Worksheet
As you work through the TO-DO LIST, you'll be filling out this worksheet.

C: Day-of Timeline
Once the big picture comes together, you'll use this template to fill out the specific logistics and timing of your day.

D: Day-of Checklist
This checklist is to make sure you don't forget anything important!

A: To-Do List

As you work through this TO-DO LIST, you should be filling out the WORKSHEET document,
while referencing this GUIDE BOOK for detailed information.

Every wedding is different, but this to-do list is meant to give you an idea of your planning workflow. Feel free to alter it as needed.

Note: While the simplicity of microweddings allows them to be planned relatively last-minute, it's best to plan your wedding as early as possible. Ultimately, it depends on your preferences. If you are set on a Saturday evening in June, many officiants and photographers may be booked 8-12 months in advance. Whereas a Tuesday morning may still have vendor/ venue options available just a couple of weeks out.

Brainstorming the Wedding
- ☐ Estimate date and time of ceremony
- ☐ Estimate guest count
- ☐ Research options for "PLACES" (ceremony site and dinner/reception site)
- ☐ Identify and research "PEOPLE" (the vendors you want to hire)

Planning the Wedding
- ☐ Confirm date and time of ceremony
- ☐ Confirm guest count (doesn't need to be exact)
- ☐ Book "PLACES"
- ☐ Book "PEOPLE"
- ☐ Figure out "CEREMONY" details (vows, religion, etc.)
- ☐ Research "LEGAL STUFF" (your officiant should help you with this)
- ☐ Address the "LITTLE STUFF"
- ☐ Complete day-of timeline and day-of checklist

Two Weeks Prior to Wedding
- ☐ Get marriage license or know exactly when/where you will be getting it
- ☐ Send email to all vendors confirming your wedding date and their arrival time
- ☐ Address any remaining vendor/venue payments that are due
- ☐ Double check the "LITTLE STUFF"

Three Days Prior to Wedding
- ☐ Check the weather forecast for ceremony site
- ☐ Double check any items that need to be picked up, such as flowers, cake, etc.
- ☐ Double check day-of checklist

Day-of Wedding
- ☐ Go through the day-of checklist!

B: Worksheet

As you work through the TO-DO LIST document, you should be filling out this WORKSHEET, while referencing this GUIDE BOOK for detailed information.

This worksheet is intended as a work tool to use throughout your planning process. Feel free to edit or add to it as needed, as every microwedding is different.

Your goal should be to complete this worksheet as you plan your wedding. You'll notice it is organized the same way as the planning guide so you can easily cross reference them.

Start with the Basics

Before you dive in, you'll want to come up with estimates for these three things, as they will likely play a huge role in your search and planning process. Don't worry about these being set in stone right away, and feel free to update them as your plans become solidified.

Wedding Date: _____

Guest Count: _____

Budget: _____

Places

Ceremony Site

Name:

Address:

Contact person:

Email:

Phone:

Website:

Time reserved:

Price:

Paid:

Dinner/Reception Site

Name:

Address:

Contact person:

Email:

Phone:

Website:

Time reserved:

Price:

Paid:

People

Officiant

Name:

Email:

Phone:

Website:

Day-of arrival time:

Price:

Paid:

Photographer

Name:

Email:

Phone:

Website:

Day-of arrival/departure time:

Price:

Paid:

Videographer

Name:

Email:

Phone:

Website:

Day-of arrival/departure time:

Price:

Paid:

Florist

Name:

Email:

Phone:

Website:

Pick-up/delivery:

Price:

Paid:

Bakery

Name:

Email:

Phone:

Website:

Pick-up/delivery:

Price:

Paid:

Hair and Makeup Stylist

Name:

Email:

Phone:

Website:

Day-of arrival time:

Price:

Paid:

Catering/Private Chef

Name:

Email:

Phone:

Website:

Day-of arrival time:

Price:

Paid:

Live Music/DJ

Name:

Email:

Phone:

Website:

Day-of arrival time:

Price:

Paid:

Bartender

Name:

Email:

Phone:

Website:

Day-of arrival time:

Price:

Paid:

Rentals, Decorator, etc.

Name:

Email:

Phone:

Website:

Day-of arrival time:

Price:

Paid:

Day-of Coordinator

Name:

Email:

Phone:

Website:

Day-of arrival time:

Price:

Paid:

Ceremony

Processional Walking Order

First:

Second:

Third:

Fourth:

Fifth:

Sixth:

Seventh:

Eighth:

Ninth:

Tenth:

Elements of Ceremony

Vows (who will have them?):

Unity ceremony:

Readings:

Rings (who will have them?):

Music

Person in charge:

Playlist for before the ceremony begins:

Processional song for the bridal party/family:

Processional song for the bride:

Recessional song:

First Look

When:

Where:

Chairs

Number of seats needed:

Delivery/set-up (who and when):

Decorations

What:

Who:

When:

Weather

Backup plan:

Gear:

Legal Stuff

This is not legal advice!
Please refer to the governing body responsible for issuing your marriage license
for specific requirements and information.

Getting the Marriage License

Where are you getting it:

When are you getting it:

What do you need to bring:

Completing the Marriage License

Witnesses (if needed):

Signing with maiden or married name:

Filing the Marriage License

Who/when/where:

Little Stuff

Rehearsal and/or Dinner Night Before Ceremony

Date:

Time:

Location:

Rehearsal:

Lodging

Location:

Dates reserved:

Weekend Plans

Friday night:

Sunday morning:

etc.

Emergency Kit

Umbrella

Extra shoes (outdoor-friendly, flip-flops, etc.)

Clothes pins

Stain remover

Lint roller

Bobby pins

Breath mints

Duct tape

Deodorant

Cash

Mini first aid kit

Phone charger/battery pack

Tissues

_____

_____

(*.you know your situation better than me - add accordingly!*)

C: Day-Of Timeline

This blank template is for you to use for your early brainstorming. Depending on the logistics of your day, you may need a lot more (or less) space. With my online toolkit you'll find a template that can be easily adjusted to fit your needs.
Information and example timelines can be found on the following pages.

Getting Ready

_____ -

_____ -

_____ -

_____ -

_____ -

_____ -

Ceremony and Photos

_____ -

_____ -

_____ -

Dinner and Reception

_____ -

_____ -

_____ -

_____ -

_____ -

_____ -

Microwedding Timeline Overview

While microweddings are generally simpler than a traditional wedding, they differ in their day-of logistics and timeline. The notes below are meant to give a *rough* idea of what a common microwedding may look like. That being said, depending on the specifics of your wedding, the timeline could vary widely.

Keep in mind, there are no hard rules! If you'd like to get all the photos out of the way before the ceremony, that's absolutely an option. The most important thing is to **work with your vendors**. Don't assume the times suggested here fit perfectly for your situation. Your photographer will work with you to determine when the photos will be taken and for how long. Your stylist will tell you how much time to allot for getting your hair and makeup done. And so on.

Generally speaking, **the more detailed your timeline is, the better**. It's your wedding day! You don't want to have to cut any aspect short or have to worry about running behind. Even for a super simple wedding, a timeline will, at the very least, offer a nice peace of mind.

Note: If your wedding has slowly evolved from "a few friends and our parents" to "pretty much everyone we know," the timeline you will likely need for coordinating a wedding of that size is out of the scope of this guide. Though this may still be a good place to start!

General Day-of Timeline Breakdown

- **Getting Ready**
  For some microweddings, this might just mean getting dressed and doing hair and makeup at home. For others, it could be stopping by a salon. And for others still, it could mean getting ready with a bridal party at the venue and

having hair and makeup stylists come to you. Whatever "getting ready" will mean for your wedding, be sure to allot enough time for it.

- **First Look**
  If the couple wants to, they can have a "first look" prior to the ceremony. Usually about 20 minutes before the ceremony, the photographer will take photos as they see each other for the first time the day of the wedding.

- **Ceremony**
  For a super simple microwedding in the park, the couple can usually arrive 15-20 minutes before the ceremony, which typically lasts about 10-15 minutes. For a more elaborate microwedding (with a larger group, seated guests, readings, processional, etc.) expect to arrive at least 30 minutes before the ceremony, which would typically last about 20 minutes (allot for 30 to be safe). But this all really depends on where you're getting ready, when you're doing photos, etc.

- **Family and group photos**
  While they can be done prior to the ceremony, for a microwedding generally, the photographer will take family and group photos immediately following the ceremony. How long this will last will depend on how many people there are and how many group shots you want. Your photographer may send you a shot list in advance, but either way you should know the specific group photos you want. This will save time, giving you more time with the photographer.

- **Couple's Portrait Session**
  Though a couple's portrait session can be done earlier in the day, they are most commonly done following the family and group photos that immediately follow the ceremony. This generally lasts about 30-45 minutes.

- **Cocktail Hour**
  For a simple microwedding with a post-ceremony dinner at a restaurant, this doesn't really apply. A traditional "cocktail hour" is where your guests can hang out during the portrait session, or after the ceremony and before the reception. For a more traditional microwedding, the guests might head to the reception location early for drinks and/or appetizers. For an intimate ceremony in the park followed by dinner downtown, guests might just wait 20 minutes or so for the couple's portrait session to end before everyone heads to dinner together.

- **Dinner/Reception**
  The dinner/reception typically caps off the day. If you are in a space that allows, feel free to plan for speeches/toasts, a first dance, cake cutting, etc.

Questions Your Timeline Should Answer

Use these questions to make sure you have all the essential bases covered when drafting your own timeline! Again, all of these questions won't apply to every wedding, and you may have additional questions that your personalized timeline should answer.

Getting Ready
- ☐ Where at?
- ☐ With who?
- ☐ When will you start?
- ☐ When will you finish?
- ☐ When do you need to leave? Account for traffic!
- ☐ Who has the cake?
- ☐ Who has the flowers?
- ☐ Who has the marriage license?
- ☐ Who has the rings?
- ☐ Anyone setting up or decorating?
- ☐ What vendors are present? Stylist? Photographer?
- ☐ ...When are they arriving?

Ceremony and Photos
- ☐ When does the couple need to arrive?
- ☐ When does the bridal party need to arrive?
- ☐ When will the guests be arriving?
- ☐ Who has the flowers?
- ☐ Who has the marriage license?
- ☐ Who has the rings?
- ☐ Photos before the ceremony? First look, bridal party, etc.
- ☐ When does the ceremony start?
- ☐ What vendors are present? Officiant? Photographer? Violinist?
- ☐ ...When are they arriving?
- ☐ When will the ceremony end?
- ☐ When will you sign the marriage license?
- ☐ Photos after the ceremony? Couple's portrait session, family, etc.
- ☐ Where do guests go during the couple's portrait session?

Dinner/Reception
- ☐ When does dinner start? Account for travel time if in a different location!
- ☐ Where is dinner?
- ☐ Anything before dinner? Cocktail hour?
- ☐ What vendors are present? Caterer? Bartender?
- ☐ ...When are they arriving?
- ☐ Who's in charge of the music?
- ☐ When are the toasts? Cake cutting? First dance?
- ☐ What time does the reception end?
- ☐ Going out to bars after? The bowling alley? Rental home?

Day Before the Wedding*
- ☐ When/where is the rehearsal/dinner?
- ☐ Is someone picking up/delivering the cake? Who? When?
- ☐ Is someone picking up/delivering flowers? Who? When?
- ☐ Are you picking up the marriage license? When? Where?
- ☐ Are you checking into a hotel? When? Where?

Obviously not part of the day-of timeline, but it never hurts to lay out a schedule for the day before the wedding!

Sample Timeline - Elopement

Getting Ready
2:00 pm - Hair and makeup stylist arrives at hotel
3:00 pm - Couple gets dressed
3:30 pm - Couple leaves hotel for park

Ceremony and Photos
3:45 pm - Couple arrives at park with marriage license, rings and flowers
3:45 pm - Officiant and photographer arrive at park
4:00 pm - Ceremony begins
4:15 pm - Ceremony concludes
4:15 pm - Bride and groom sign the marriage license
4:15 pm - Couple's portrait session begins
5:00 pm - Portrait session ends
5:00 pm - Couple leaves for dinner

Dinner and Reception
5:30 pm - Couple arrives at dinner reservation

Sample Timeline - Microwedding (Casual)

Getting Ready

1:00 pm - The couple and bridal party arrive at rental home and start getting ready

1:30 pm - Hair and makeup stylists arrive and begin with bridal party

1:30 pm - Flowers are delivered

3:00 pm - The couple and bridal party finish getting ready and leave for beach

Ceremony and Photos

2:45 pm - Rental company delivers and sets up chairs at beach

3:30 pm - Guests begin arriving at beach (mother of bride has marriage license)

3:30 pm - The couple and bridal party arrive at beach (best man has rings)

3:40 pm - The couple have a "first look" with the photographer

4:00 pm - Ceremony begins

4:30 pm - Ceremony ends

4:30 pm - Group and family photos begin

5:00 pm - Guests and bridal party leave for restaurant

5:00 pm - Couple's portrait session begins

5:30 pm - Couple's portrait session ends

5:30 pm - Couple leaves for restaurant

Dinner and Reception

6:00 pm - Couple arrives at dinner

6:15 pm - Best man and/or maid of honor toast

8:00 pm - Cake cutting (Aunt Rosa will pick up cake morning-of)

9:00 pm - Back to rental home for after party

Sample Timeline - Microwedding (Traditional)

Getting Ready
10:00 am - Decorators and/or family members arrive at venue for set up
12:00 pm - Couple and bridal party arrive at venue (with marriage license and rings)
12:00 pm - Photographer arrives at venue for "getting ready" photos
12:30 pm - Hair and makeup stylists arrive and begin with bridal party
12:30 pm - Flowers delivered
12:30 pm - Cake delivered
3:00 pm - The couple and bridal party finish getting ready

Ceremony and Photos
3:15 pm - The couple has their "first look" with the photographer
3:30 pm - Bridal party and family photos
3:30 pm - DJ arrives for set up
3:30 pm - Bartender arrives for set up
3:45 pm - Officiant arrives
4:00 pm - Guests start arriving
4:00 pm - Caterer arrives for set up
4:15 pm - The couple and bridal party line up for processional
4:30 pm - Ceremony begins
5:00 pm - Ceremony ends
5:00 pm - Cocktail hour begins
5:00 pm - Guests go inside
5:05 pm - Couple signs marriage license with officiant, best man, and maid of honor
5:15 pm - Couple's portrait session begins
6:00 pm - Portrait session ends, cocktail hour ends, begin seating for dinner

Dinner and Reception
6:15 pm - Dinner buffet line starts
7:00 pm - Toasts begin
7:30 pm - Cake cut and served
8:00 pm - First dance / Party
11:00 pm - Guests leave, begin clean up
11:30 pm - Everyone must be out, venue doors locked

D: Day-Of Checklist

This checklist is for you to have with you the day of the wedding. This should cover the "necessities" but feel free to add to it as needed!

Weather forecast: _____

- ☐ Vendor payments
- ☐ Ceremony site permit
- ☐ Marriage license
- ☐ Vows
- ☐ Rings
- ☐ Flowers
- ☐ Cake
- ☐ Emergency kit
- ☐ Printed version of day-of checklist, timeline, and worksheet

NEED MORE HELP?

- **"How To Officiate a Wedding" e-guide - $50**
  1-on-1 coaching and resources to help anyone officiate!
  MicroWeddings.org/Coaching

- **Remote Planning Assistance - $50**
  Let's hop on a phone call! I'll help you brainstorm and figure out your day.
  MicroWeddings.org/Remote

- **All-Inclusive MicroWedding Planning - $325ish**
  From the mountaintop, to the photographer and officiant, I'll help you put together every single piece of your day! (Currently only available for weddings in Colorado)
  ColoradoMicroWeddings.com

- **Wedding Officiant - $400 + Travel**
  It would be my absolute honor to officiate your ceremony! I do weddings of all shapes and sizes, and travel anywhere in the world.
  Iver@MicroWeddings.org

- **Blog Posts, Articles, Videos, Podcasts...**
  All sorts of fun stuff. :-)
  MicroWeddings.org

ABOUT THE AUTHOR

Iver Marjerison

Iver Marjerison (founder of MicroWeddings.org) is a professional wedding planner and officiant who specializes in small weddings, elopements, and "micro-weddings". He has personally planned more than 500 weddings, and holds a 5-star rating for his services on WeddingWire.com and TheKnot.com, where he has earned the "Best of Weddings" award 3 years in a row. Beyond his work as a wedding planner, he has written and published a food guidebook series "The Foodist Bucket List", hosts the "Do New" podcast, is the creator of the card game "Drink" and the board game "Fate's Folly" (release date 2021), and spent a year doing one new thing every week (Youtube.com/DoNew).

Iver@MicroWeddings.org
IG: @Iver.Marjerison
IverMarjerison.com

If for any reason you are not 100% satisfied with this guide, please reach out for a full refund.

CPSIA information can be obtained
at www.ICGtesting.com
Printed in the USA
BVHW042055230921
617413BV00016B/1362